Spotlight on™ Reading & Listening (
Paraphrasing & Sun

by Paul F. Johnson & Carolyn LoGiudice

Skills	Ages
■ reading	■ 11 and up
■ listening	**Grades**
	■ 6 and up

Evidence-Based Practice

■ Explicitly teaching and reinforcing inference-making leads to better outcomes in overall text comprehension, text engagement, and metacognitive thinking (Borné, Cox, Hartgering, & Pratt, 2005).

■ Summarization is a skill that helps students identify main ideas, generalize what they've read, and recall information needed to answer comprehension questions (NRP, 2000).

■ Instruction in comprehension can help students understand, remember, and communicate with others about what they read (NIFL, 2003).

■ Teacher questioning improves students' learning from reading because it gives them a purpose for reading, focuses their attention on what they are to learn, helps them think actively as they read, encourages them to monitor their comprehension, and helps them review content and relate what they've learned to what they already know (NIFL, 2003).

■ Effective listening strategies include (NCLRC, 2004):
  • Listening for details and main ideas   • Summarizing
  • Predicting   • Recognizing word-order patterns
  • Drawing inferences

Spotlight on Reading & Listening Comprehension Level 2 incorporates these principles and is also based on expert professional practice.

References
Borné, L., Cox, J., Hartgering, M., & Pratt, E. (2005). *Making inferences from text* [Overview]. Dorchester, MA: Project for School Innovation.

National Capital Language Resource Center (NCLRC). (2004). *Strategies for developing listening skills.* Retrieved June 15, 2009, from www.nclrc.org/essentials/listening/stratlisten.htm

National Institute for Literacy (NIFL). (2003). *Put reading first: The research building blocks for teaching children to read.* Retrieved June 15, 2009, from www.nifl.gov/nifl/publications.html

National Reading Panel (NRP). (2000). *Teaching children to read: An evidence-based assessment of the scientific research literature on reading and its implications for reading instruction–Reports of the subgroups.* Retrieved June 15, 2009, from http://www.nichd.nih.gov/publications/nrp/upload/smallbook_pdf.pdf

LinguiSystems

LinguiSystems, Inc.
3100 4th Avenue
East Moline, IL 61244
800-776-4332

FAX: 800-577-4555
Email: service@linguisystems.com
Web: linguisystems.com

Printed in the U.S.A.
ISBN 978-0-7606-0735-0

About the Authors

Paul F. Johnson, B.A., and **Carolyn LoGiudice**, M.S., CCC-SLP, are editors and writers for LinguiSystems. They have collaborated to develop several publications, including *Story Comprehension To Go*, *No-Glamour Sequencing Cards*, and *Spotlight on Reasoning & Problem Solving*. Paul and Carolyn share a special interest in boosting students' language, critical thinking, and academic skills.

In their spare time, Paul and Carolyn enjoy their families, music, gourmet cooking, and reading. Paul, a proud father of three children, also enjoys bicycling, playing music, and spending rare moments alone with his wife, Kenya. Carolyn is learning to craft greeting cards and spoil grandchildren.

Cover design by Jeff Taylor

Editing and page layout by Karen Stontz

Table of Contents

Introduction

Spotlight on Reading & Listening Comprehension was developed in 2005 to provide controlled reading materials for improving both overall and specific comprehension skills. Six separate booklets presented passages with readabilities that varied from grades 2.0 through 4.9 along with follow-up comprehension questions. Each booklet focused on one of these key reading comprehension skills:

- Characters & Actions
- Comparing & Contrasting
- Figurative Language & Exclusion

- Making Inferences & Drawing Conclusions
- Paraphrasing & Summarizing
- Sequencing & Problem Solving

Requests for a similar approach to reading comprehension skill-building that would be more appealing to older students has resulted in *Spotlight on Reading & Listening Comprehension, Level 2*. Not only are the readabilities of the passages increased in this series, but the content and visual elements are designed to appeal to older students reading below grade level.

Each booklet includes stories and comprehension questions for detecting the main idea, identifying details, and thinking about the vocabulary and semantics in the passage. In addition, each booklet includes comprehension questions for a specific skill area. This particular booklet features questions that require students to paraphrase or summarize what they have read. The other five booklets focus on these skill areas:

- Comparing & Contrasting
- Understanding Everyday Information
- Figurative Language

- Fact & Opinion
- Making Inferences & Drawing Conclusions

The readability of the passages is controlled, based on the Flesch-Kincaid readability statistics. These statistics were revised in 2002; the new statistics yield a higher grade level in most cases than the previous ones. The range in readability is from grade levels 4.0 through 6.9. Each booklet includes eleven passages with the following readability ranges:

- Passages 1-3   Readability 4.0-4.9
- Passages 4-7   Readability 5.0-5.9
- Passages 8-11   Readability 6.0-6.9

The question pages for each passage also ask students to formulate questions about what they have read. The last task for each passage is a related writing prompt.

Use these passages for groups of students or individuals. Photocopy the material so each student has a copy. Encourage your students to highlight or underline key information as they read each passage and to jot down any questions they have.

Research proves that repeated readings improve reading comprehension and that three reads are usually sufficient repetition for a student to grasp the content, assuming a passage is at or below the student's reading competency level. We recommend training students to read a passage three times for adequate comprehension before trying to answer the comprehension questions.

The reading comprehension questions are similar to those found on classroom and national reading comprehension tests. Have your students read each possible answer for the multiple-choice questions before they select their answers.

As you present information to your students, model your own reading comprehension strategies. Talk about ways to rescan a passage to find key information and other tips that will help your students improve their reading competence and confidence.

We hope you will find *Spotlight on Reading & Listening Comprehension, Level 2* a welcome resource to help students understand and find satisfaction in what they read.

Paul and Carolyn

Story 1

Terrell hates being in the marching band, but his mom won't let him quit. She keeps reminding him how much she paid for his trumpet. She says, "I didn't spend $800 so you could just give it up after two years."

It's not playing the trumpet Terrell dislikes. He loves playing music with a group. He just can't stand the marching practice. His school's band has won many awards, and it takes its marching seriously. The band members practice for an hour before school starts and then again after school. That's in addition to the regular band period.

Terrell would rather spend his time playing music. He didn't know what to do about his problem until he remembered the school's jazz band. The jazz band members never march. They just stand on the stage and play. Another great thing about the jazz band is that it only practices during school. That would leave him time to do other things during the day. He only hopes he can convince his mom that joining the jazz band will be a great idea.

Main Idea and Details

1. What is the main idea of this story?

    a. Terrell is an excellent trumpet player.

    b. Terrell wants to quit the marching band.

    c. Terrell's mom doesn't like the jazz band.

2. How much did Terrell's mom pay for his trumpet?

    a. $800

    b. $1,000

    c. She got it free.

3. Which group does Terrell want to join?

    a. orchestra

    b. marching band

    c. jazz band

Vocabulary and Semantics

4. Terrell can't stand marching band practice. Which of these means the opposite of **can't stand**?

    a. dislikes

    b. takes care of

    c. enjoys

5. The jazz band practices during school. What is another word for **practices**?

    a. rehearses

    b. ignores

    c. teaches

Paraphrasing and Summarizing

6. Which sentence is a good summary of this story?

    a. Terrell wants to quit marching band because he doesn't like playing the trumpet.

    b. Terrell wants to switch instruments so he can join the jazz band.

    c. Terrell likes playing music in a group, but he doesn't like the marching band.

7. **Terrell's marching band takes its marching seriously.** What is another way to say that?

    a. The band instructor yells at the kids.

    b. The band practices a lot so it plays well.

    c. If the band doesn't win awards, it will be shut down.

8. **The jazz band only practices during school.** What does that mean?

    a. The jazz band practices the same hours as the marching band.

    b. The jazz band practices before and after school.

    c. The jazz band doesn't practice outside of school hours.

Asking Questions

Ask a question about playing an instrument.

Writing and Discussion Prompt ································

What instrument would you like to play? Give three reasons you chose this instrument. If you aleady play an instrument, tell what instrument you would play instead and why.

Story 2

Photo courtesy of istockphoto.com © Franky Sze

What do you get when you take a bunch of kids from the inner city and put them in the forest? You might end up with a lot of very bored and extremely unhappy kids. This group wasn't all that pleased at first, but they ended up having an excellent time together.

Thirty kids from Woodson Homes hit the trail for a week of hiking and camping. "I couldn't get to sleep," one camper said. "It was just too quiet and peaceful out there. I'm used to traffic, sirens, and other street sounds. It took me two nights before I could get any real sleep. But after that I slept like a log!"

Every year a different group of city kids takes part in this program. Ten adult guides help them set up campsites and then show them how to cook their meals over an open fire. At the beginning of the week, everything is new to the kids. By the last day, though, they're ready to take care of themselves.

For most of the campers, this is their first trip outside of their neighborhood. The trip is a great way to give kids new experiences.

Main Idea and Details

1. Which of these doesn't tell the main idea of the story?

    a. City kids spend a week in the woods.

    b. Kids from the city have a good time camping.

    c. Camping isn't a good activity for everyone.

2. How many kids went on this trip?

    a. 60

    b. 30

    c. 10

3. Does the same group of kids go camping every year?

    a. yes

    b. no

    c. The story doesn't say.

Vocabulary and Semantics

4. The story says that the kids hit the trail for a week of hiking and camping. What does **hit the trail** mean?

    a. They went to the woods.

    b. They walked several miles to the campsite.

    c. They slept on the trail.

5. One camper says she **slept like a log**. What does that mean?

    a. She had a hard time sleeping.

    b. She slept very well.

    c. She slept next to a tree.

Paraphrasing and Summarizing

6. What is a good summary of this story?

    a. It is difficult for city kids to sleep in the woods.

    b. Kids from the city had a good camping experience.

    c. Some people don't like to get away from their neighborhood.

7. One camper said that **it took her two nights before she could get any real sleep**. What is another way to say that?

    a. She didn't sleep very well during the trip.

    b. She slept well on the third night.

    c. She slept well on the first night.

8. **By the last day, the kids were ready to take care of themselves**. What is another way to say that?

    a. The kids knew what they were doing by the end of the trip.

    b. Some of the kids never learned how to take care of themselves.

    c. Most kids knew what they were doing right away.

Asking Questions

Ask a question about camping in the woods.

Writing and Discussion Prompt ·····································

Imagine you are going on a camping trip. Not counting clothes or food, what three things from home would you need to bring along?

Story 3

Photo courtesy of istockphoto.com © JoeStark

Everyone in the world is looking for new ways to create power without oil. Energy from the wind might not be the answer, but it could be a start. Wind farms are popping up all over the world. A wind farm is a large group of wind turbines in one spot. When the air moves all those big blades, it generates electricity. That power then goes to homes and businesses.

Making electricity from the wind used to be expensive. New technology and huge wind farms have brought those costs down.

Not everyone agrees that wind power is a good idea. Some people think the huge turbines are ugly. They can also kill birds in flight. If a turbine isn't placed correctly, it can even interfere with TV and radio signals. The biggest argument against wind farms might be the wind itself. We can't turn it on and off, so we can't predict when the blades on the big towers will spin.

Most people agree that power from the wind is cheap and clean. Some also believe that the wind is an unpredictable power source.

Main Idea and Details

1. What is the main idea of this story?

   a. People have different ideas about wind energy.

   b. Wind energy is the solution to our energy problems.

   c. Wind energy is free.

2. Which of these isn't a problem with wind energy?

   a. It can harm birds in flight.

   b. It can interfere with TV and radio signals.

   c. It is a clean form of energy.

3. Wind energy used to be _____.

   a. expensive

   b. noisy

   c. safe

Vocabulary and Semantics

4. What is a **wind farm**?

   a. a place to grow plants that need wind to survive

   b. many wind turbines in one place

   c. an area where the wind blows all the time

5. Some people think wind turbines are ugly. Which word doesn't mean the same as **ugly**?

   a. unsightly

   b. attractive

   c. nasty

Paraphrasing and Summarizing

6. Which sentence summarizes why some people are in favor of wind energy?

   a. Wind turbines are beautiful.

   b. It is a cheap, clean source of energy.

   c. Wind energy is reliable.

7. The story says **not everyone thinks wind power is a good idea**. What is another way to say that?

   a. Almost everyone thinks wind energy is a good idea.

   b. Wind energy is very reliable.

   c. Some people are not in favor of wind energy.

8. The story says **we can't predict when the blades on the big towers will spin**. What is another way to say that?

   a. We aren't able to control the wind.

   b. The wind blows constantly.

   c. We can turn the blades on and off.

Asking Questions

Ask a question about generating electricity from the wind.

Writing and Discussion Prompt ·····························

Imagine you are designing a vehicle that runs on wind power. What would it look like? What problems could you have with the vehicle?

Story 4

Carla and Mario are having some serious problems. They've been friends since first grade, but lately all they've done is argue. They can't talk for five minutes without fighting.

Mario is tired of Carla telling him what to do. He thinks she treats him like a baby. Carla thinks Mario is hanging out with a bunch of losers who will only bring him trouble. She thinks she has to warn him before anything bad happens.

They have never argued like this before, but since they began eighth grade, almost every time they talk, an argument starts.

It hasn't all been bad, though. Mario was the first one at Carla's door when her little brother was rushed to the hospital for emergency surgery. Carla talked on the phone with Mario for hours when he was having trouble with his dad. These two will always be friends, but their friendship is changing. They aren't little kids anymore. The way they talk to each other will be different from now on. Even if they fight, Carla and Mario know that they will always be there for one another.

Main Idea and Details

1. What is the main idea of this story?

   a. Fighting with friends is a bad idea.

   b. Carla and Mario's friendship is changing.

   c. Friendships sometimes break up.

2. How long have Carla and Mario been friends?

   a. since the beginning of eighth grade

   b. since middle school

   c. since first grade

3. Who went to the hospital for emergency surgery?

   a. Carla's little brother

   b. Mario's dad

   c. Mario

Vocabulary and Semantics

4. **Mario thinks Carla treats him like a baby.** What does that mean?

   a. He cries a lot.

   b. They can't get along at all.

   c. She doesn't think he can make his own decisions.

5. Carla thinks Mario is hanging out with a bunch of losers. What are **losers**?

   a. troublemakers

   b. people with good ideas

   c. good students

Paraphrasing and Summarizing

6. Which sentence summarizes this story?

    a. Even though they fight, Carla and Mario are still friends.

    b. Carla and Mario are no longer good friends.

    c. Carla and Mario will always fight.

7. **Carla and Mario can't talk for five minutes without fighting**. What is another way to say that?

    a. Carla and Mario don't talk much.

    b. Carla and Mario are enemies.

    c. Carla and Mario fight a lot.

8. **Carla and Mario aren't little kids anymore**. What is another way to say that?

    a. They don't play with toys.

    b. They are growing up.

    c. They don't spend much time together.

Asking Questions

Ask a question about arguing with a friend.

Writing and Discussion Prompt ·······························

What things do you think most friends argue about? What can friends do to make up after an argument?

Story 5

Even dogs have their own kind of Olympics. It's called "dog agility," and it's a way for dogs to compete as athletes.

A dog agility contest is a special obstacle course where dogs go up and down ramps, over jumps, and through tunnels. These dogs aren't on leashes, and they don't get treats. Their trainers can only use hand and voice signals to guide them.

Dogs of all sizes enter the contests, but the smaller, faster dogs are often the most popular. Crowds love to watch these tiny dogs sprint through the course and jump the highest bars. That's probably because these furry athletes seem to be having such a great time themselves! Some people think they can even see these dogs smiling as they work through the course.

It takes a lot of work to get ready for dog agility. Trainers spend hours every day with their dogs, but they'll all tell you it's worth it. All of that working together creates a special bond between a dog and a person.

Main Idea and Details

1. What is the main idea of this story?

    a. Trainers spend hours with their dogs.

    b. Dogs and their trainers take part in dog agility contests.

    c. Small dogs love to run obstacle courses.

2. Which of these don't trainers give dogs during the contest?

    a. hand signals

    b. treats

    c. voice signals

3. Which kind of dogs do crowds like to watch best?

    a. small, fast dogs

    b. large, strong dogs

    c. medium-sized, furry dogs

Vocabulary and Semantics

4. Which of these describes an Olympics?

    a. an athletic contest

    b. a special game

    c. an obstacle course

5. People like to watch tiny dogs sprint through the course. Which of these words doesn't mean the same as **sprint**?

    a. dash

    b. race

    c. stumble

Paraphrasing and Summarizing

6. Which sentence best summarizes this story?

   a. Olympics for dogs and people are alike.

   b. Dogs have to run the course without treats.

   c. A dog and its trainer have to work well together in dog agility.

7. What is another way to say **dogs of all sizes enter the contest**?

   a. Most people like to watch small dogs compete.

   b. Different-sized dogs compete in dog agility.

   c. The dogs in the contest seem to be having fun.

8. What is another way to say **trainers spend hours every day with their dogs**?

   a. Dogs and trainers spend a lot of time together.

   b. Smaller dogs are harder to train.

   c. Dog agility is something most dogs enjoy.

Asking Questions

Ask a question about training a dog.

Writing and Discussion Prompt ······································

Imagine you are going to hold a people agility competition. What things would you have people do during the contest? What obstacles would you put up?

Story 6

What makes someone an artist? Does an artist have to go to college and have years of training, or can anyone make art? Those are questions people have been asking for over a hundred years. Art that is made by ordinary people is called folk art, and it comes in many forms. One of the newest forms of folk art is graffiti.

Graffiti is found all over: bridges, train cars, and storefront doors are all places for graffiti artists to leave their tags. A tag is often just the artist's street name, but some tags are gang names or special symbols. The best graffiti artists take their work far beyond tagging. They create little masterpieces of color and form.

No matter how beautiful graffiti can be, there is a problem. It's illegal to paint on property that isn't your own. Some cities have declared war on graffiti. They have special police squads who arrest graffiti artists. Other communities have handled things differently. They try to find the most talented artists and put them to work. They hire them to create murals and paintings in public places. That solution keeps both the city and its graffiti artists very happy.

Main Idea and Details

1. What would be a good title for this story?

    a. Graffiti Problems and Solutions

    b. Tagging Isn't Art

    c. Declaring War on Graffiti

2. What type of art is graffiti?

    a. museum art

    b. bad art

    c. folk art

3. Where do you find graffiti?

    a. on places like bridges, train cars, and storefront doors

    b. in art galleries

    c. on the Internet

Vocabulary and Semantics

4. What is **folk art**?

    a. art made by ordinary people

    b. illegal art

    c. art made in cities

5. Ordinary people create folk art. Which word means the opposite of **ordinary**?

    a. regular

    b. rare

    c. everyday

Paraphrasing and Summarizing

6. Which sentence does not summarize a part of this story?

   a. Ordinary people can make interesting art.

   b. You need a lot of spray paint to make graffiti.

   c. Some graffiti artists are very talented.

7. What is the biggest problem with graffiti?

   a. It is illegal to paint graffiti on private property.

   b. Graffiti artists need special training.

   c. Most graffiti isn't that well done.

8. Some cities have found a solution that keeps both the city and its graffiti artists happy. What is that solution?

   a. The cities have special police squads who arrest graffiti artists.

   b. The cities hire the most talented graffiti artists to create wall paintings in public places.

   c. The cities allow the graffiti artists to paint wherever they want to.

Asking Questions

Ask a question about making art.

Writing and Discussion Prompt ···································

What do you think about graffiti? Do you think it is interesting and cool or just messy?

Story 7

Many animals thrive in zoos, but it may be different for elephants. Elephants in the wild are creatures that need to roam. They spend their days traveling miles as a family group. In zoos, they are often kept in small enclosures with little room to move naturally. Because of their size and need to wander, a zoo might not be the best place for them. As a result, groups have been calling for zoos to set their elephants free.

Some large zoos are taking that advice and acting on it. They are finding that elephants are not very happy or healthy in their confined homes, so they are sending them to wild animal parks. They have huge areas there for the elephants to explore.

Elephants are fascinating, gentle animals. People love to visit them, but it's beginning to look like the zoo might not be the best place to do that. People can still see them at a wild animal park, but they may not be able to get as close to them as they did in zoos. Most people want to find a way to both enjoy the elephants and keep them healthy.

Main Idea and Details

1. What is the main idea of this story?

    a. Elephants need a lot of food.

    b. Elephants might not be happy in zoos.

    c. Elephants try to escape from zoos.

2. Where are some zoos sending their elephants?

    a. the circus

    b. wild animal parks

    c. back to the wild

3. What do elephants need that zoos cannot provide?

    a. large areas of land

    b. food

    c. a safe place to live

Vocabulary and Semantics

4. Elephants are creatures that need to roam. What is another word for **creatures**?

    a. animals

    b. babies

    c. cages

5. **Elephants have a need to roam**. What does that mean?

    a. They need a lot of space to move around.

    b. Elephants are happy in confined areas.

    c. Elephants are never kept in cages.

Paraphrasing and Summarizing

6. Which sentence best summarizes this story?

    a. It is difficult to see elephants in a zoo.

    b. Elephants are the most important animals in a zoo.

    c. People want to see elephants, but they want them to be happy.

7. **Many animals thrive in zoos**. What is another way to say that?

    a. A zoo is not a good place for animals to live.

    b. Many animals are healthy and happy in zoos.

    c. It takes a lot of work to run a zoo.

8. **Elephants are not happy in their confined homes**. What is another way to say that?

    a. Zoos give elephants large areas for roaming.

    b. Everyone wants elephants to stay confined.

    c. Most elephants are happy in open spaces.

Asking Questions

Ask a question about elephants.

Writing and Discussion Prompt ································

Imagine you had an elephant for a pet. What things would you do to take care of it?

Story 8

A block sale is a great way to make some money and find bargains at the same time. A block sale can go by a lot of different names. You might know it better as a rummage sale, a yard sale, or a tag sale. It doesn't matter what you call it, the idea is the same.

In a block sale, a lot of people come together in one place to sell their old stuff. People from the same neighborhood or organization will often get together and have a large block sale. Some people end up making money during the sale, but others spend as much as or more than they make.

When you're selling stuff at a block sale, it's hard not to look around at the things other people have brought. You might find that perfect picture frame, a cool old lamp, or a DVD you've been looking for. Before you know it, you're swiping money from your own cash box to spend on things you think you can't live without.

Nobody is ever going to get rich selling items at a block sale. The event is mostly about earning a little money, spending time with people, and, if you're lucky, finding a great bargain.

Main Idea and Details

1. What is the main idea of this story?

    a. You can lose a lot of money at a block sale.

    b. A block sale is a good place to buy a DVD.

    c. People buy and sell things at a block sale.

2. Which item is not mentioned in the story?

    a. picture frame

    b. CD

    c. lamp

3. What is something that doesn't happen at a block sale?

    a. People order food.

    b. People buy things.

    c. People sell things.

Vocabulary and Semantics

4. Which of these is not another way to say **block sale**?

    a. rummage sale

    b. clearance sale

    c. tag sale

5. The story mentions swiping money from your own cash box. Which word means the opposite of **swiping**?

    a. giving

    b. stealing

    c. taking

Paraphrasing and Summarizing

6. What is a good way to summarize what happens to many people at a block sale?

    a. They find a cool lamp.

    b. They sell and buy things.

    c. They get rich from the things they sell.

7. What is a way to describe something that is a **bargain**?

    a. a good price for something you don't want or need

    b. something you want at a good price

    c. a useful item at an expensive price

8. What is another way to say **things you can't live without**?

    a. things that help you breathe

    b. unnecessary things

    c. things you need

Asking Questions

Ask a question about a block sale.

Writing and Discussion Prompt ....

Imagine you are going to sell some of your things at a block sale. What three things would you sell, and what price would you put on each thing? Why did you choose those three things?

Story 9

Some form of pizza has been one of the world's favorite foods for hundreds of years. Everywhere you go, it's a little bit different, but the basics of pizza stay the same. It all starts with a bread-like crust that is topped with some sort of sauce. A layer of cheese usually finishes off a pizza before it's popped into an oven.

The kind of pizza you eat also depends on where you live. Chicago is famous for its deep-dish pizza. Chicago pizza has a very thick crust, tons of sauce and toppings, and a thick layer of cheese. Pizza in New York is the complete opposite. New Yorkers liked thin, crunchy crust with sauce, a thin layer of cheese, and often nothing else. In Chicago, people sit down to eat a whole pizza together. A New Yorker is more likely to grab a single slice on the go.

New York and Chicago are two places that have very different versions of pizza, but other cities and towns have their own styles too.

Main Idea and Details

1. What would be a good title for this story?

   a. Chicago Is a Thick Pizza Town

   b. Cheese Tops Every Pizza

   c. Different Pizzas for Different Places

2. Which three ingredients do most pizzas have?

   a. bread, sauce, and cheese

   b. crust, sauce, and cheese

   c. crust, mushrooms, and sausage

3. Which city isn't mentioned in the story?

   a. Baltimore

   b. Chicago

   c. New York

Vocabulary and Semantics

4. A pizza is popped into an oven. What does **popped** mean?

   a. removed

   b. exploded

   c. placed

5. New York pizzas have a crunchy crust. What word means the opposite of **crunchy**?

   a. crispy

   b. chewy

   c. chunky

Paraphrasing and Summarizing

6. The story says **the basics of pizza stay the same**. What is another way to say that?

   a. Most pizza contains tomato sauce.

   b. Pizza is usually made from the same basic ingredients.

   c. Every city has its own style of pizza.

7. Which sentence best describes a typical New York pizza?

   a. It has a thin crust, sauce, and cheese.

   b. It has a thick crust, sausage, and cheese.

   c. New York pizza is usually very large.

8. Which sentence summarizes the basic difference between New York and Chicago pizza?

   a. New Yorkers eat more pizza than people in Chicago do.

   b. New York pizza has thin crust and Chicago pizza has thick crust.

   c. People enjoy pizza from both New York and Chicago.

Asking Questions

Ask a question about making a pizza.

Writing and Discussion Prompt ••••••••••••••••••••••••••••••

Design "the world's weirdest pizza." What ingredients would you include? How would you prepare the pizza? Write a complete recipe for your weird pizza.

Story 10

What career do you see in your future? The kinds of jobs people do have changed a lot. Jobs that were popular in the past, like factory worker and farmer, are disappearing. Many traditional careers now require technical training.

Farming and factory work used to be pretty straightforward. It took hard physical work and long hours to get those jobs done. Now farmers use computerized equipment to grow more and better quality crops and livestock. Robots and high-tech materials in factories mean that workers need to have more skills than just strength and hard work.

Almost any job these days requires some math and computer skills. Communication is also important because now people work together to do jobs that they used to do alone.

Farming and factory work are just two jobs that have seen big changes. Teaching today is also different. A teacher used to only need a chalkboard and textbooks. Whiteboards, computers, and the Internet are now important teaching tools. All of these jobs will continue to evolve. The skills you'll need to do them will change too.

Main Idea and Details

1. What would be a good title for this story?

    a. New Skills for Old Careers

    b. Farmers Make Big Changes

    c. Robots Are the Future in Factories

2. Which career is not mentioned in the story?

    a. teacher

    b. salesperson

    c. farmer

3. Which of these are important tools for teachers today?

    a. hard work and chalkboards

    b. robots and strength

    c. computers and the Internet

Vocabulary and Semantics

4. Which of these words does not go with technology?

    a. computers

    b. robots

    c. physical

5. Farmers use computerized equipment. Which of these means the same as **equipment**?

    a. livestock

    b. machines

    c. careers

Paraphrasing and Summarizing

6. Which sentence tells how farmers used to do their jobs?

    a. They worked with their hands for long hours.

    b. They were just learning to use computers.

    c. Planting and taking care of livestock was easier.

7. Why is communication an important job skill?

    a. A job is easier if you have people to talk to.

    b. Most jobs require people to work together.

    c. Most people don't like to talk when they are working.

8. Which sentence best summarizes this story?

    a. Skills needed for jobs are always changing.

    b. Teaching has changed a lot over the years.

    c. Most jobs stay basically the same.

Asking Questions

Ask a question about one of the jobs in the story.

Writing and Discussion Prompt ·····································

Which job mentioned in the story could you see yourself doing? Why did you

choose that job? Which job would you least like to do? Why?

Story 11

Mountain biking is an exciting activity, but it can also be an extremely dangerous one for a new rider. There's nothing like hitting a challenging dirt trail, but you should be prepared before you go.

A lot of new trail riders don't know what's in store for them, because even the easiest trails can hide some big surprises. Tree roots, slippery puddles, and steep climbs are a part of almost any mountain bike trail. The best way to stay safe is to wear a helmet and be ready for anything.

Wearing a helmet is a must when you ride off-road. You should also know how to fall off your bike safely. A lot of new riders don't know how to let go of the bike and get away from it. Most injuries happen when legs and arms get tangled in bike parts. If you lose control, you should let go and fall away from your bike. Falling is a big part of mountain biking, and any rider needs to know how to do it correctly.

A twisted wheel or bent handlebar is a lot easier to fix than a broken leg, so be prepared. Mountain biking is all about adventure and exploration, but it's also about safety.

Readability 6.5
Copyright © 2007 LinguiSystems, Inc.

Main Idea and Details

1. What is the main idea of this story?

    a. Many people are afraid of mountain bike trails.

    b. Falling is an important part of bike riding.

    c. Mountain biking is exciting, but it can be dangerous.

2. Which of these is not mentioned as an important safety tip for mountain biking?

    a. wearing a helmet

    b. knowing how to fall

    c. having strong legs

3. How do most injuries happen?

    a. Legs and arms get tangled in bike parts.

    b. Bicycle brakes fail.

    c. Paths are slippery.

Vocabulary and Semantics

4. Mountain biking is dangerous for new riders. What is another word for **new**?

    a. professional

    b. inexperienced

    c. expert

5. Wearing a helmet is a must. What word means the same as **a must**?

    a. necessary

    b. optional

    c. uncomfortable

Paraphrasing and Summarizing

6. **A lot of new trail riders don't know what's in store for them.** What is another way to say that?

   a. Safety rules are hard for new riders to remember.

   b. Many new riders don't know the dangers of mountain biking.

   c. Mountain biking is easier than it looks.

7. What is the most important part of falling correctly?

   a. holding the bike closely

   b. getting away from the bike

   c. keeping your helmet in place

8. Which sentence best summarizes the message of this story?

   a. New mountain bike riders should learn basic safety.

   b. Wearing a helmet is important.

   c. Bent handlebars and twisted wheels are easy to fix.

Asking Questions

Ask a question about mountain biking.

Writing and Discussion Prompt ••••••••••••••••••••••••••••••••••

What is your favorite sport? What safety equipment should you use when you participate in that sport? How does each piece of equipment protect you?

Answer Key

Story 1
1. b
2. a
3. c
4. c
5. a
6. c
7. b
8. c

Story 2
1. c
2. b
3. b
4. a
5. b
6. b
7. b
8. a

Story 3
1. a
2. c
3. a
4. b
5. b
6. b
7. c
8. a

Story 4
1. b
2. c
3. a
4. c
5. a
6. a
7. c
8. b

Story 5
1. b
2. b
3. a
4. a
5. c
6. c
7. b
8. a

Story 6
1. a
2. c
3. a
4. a
5. b
6. b
7. a
8. b

Story 7
1. b
2. b
3. a
4. a
5. a
6. c
7. b
8. c

Story 8
1. c
2. b
3. a
4. b
5. a
6. b
7. b
8. c

Story 9
1. c
2. b
3. a
4. c
5. b
6. b
7. a
8. b

Story 10
1. a
2. b
3. c
4. c
5. b
6. a
7. b
8. a

Story 11
1. c
2. c
3. a
4. b
5. a
6. b
7. b
8. a

Spotlight on Reading & Listening Comprehension
Level 2: Paraphrasing & Summarizing

23-09-9876543

Copyright © 2007 LinguiSystems, Inc.